WITCHCRAFT FOR BEGINNERS

A SIMPLE INTRODUCTION TO MAGIC FOR THE MODERN WITCH

BRIDGET BISHOP

HENTOPAN
PUBLISHING

CONTENTS

Get this additional book free just for joining the Hentopan Launch Squad.

Hundreds of others are already enjoying early access to all of our current and future books, 100% free.
If you want insider access, plus this free book, all you have to do is scan the code below with your phone!

INTRODUCTION

For decades now, spirituality has been placed firmly in mainstream culture. The growing interest in witchcraft driven by millennials, as well as the popularity of tarot cards, candles, and crystals by way of the health and wellness industry has brought the practice of magic from the fringes of society right into your Instagram feed. For hundreds of years, the practice of witchcraft and magic has carried a negative stigma. Witches have been stereotyped and depicted in the most unflattering ways. However, these days, magical practices have gained in popularity and found their way into modern belief systems.

Witchcraft has a complicated and long history before the beauty and wellness industries more recently have become obsessed with it. As the witch aesthetic has been on the rise, so has the population of individuals who identify as witches. Practicing witch-craft is an easy transition for the many who are already involved in mindfulness, meditation, yoga, and new-age spirituality. It is necessary to note that this book is not intended to convert anyone into Wiccanism. As a matter of fact, some witches reject the current form of Wicca because it appeals to some as an imperfect reinvention of witchcraft.

As far back as the 13th century, witches have been thriving business owners offering health and wellness treatments, magical rituals, potions, and elixirs. The modern commercialization of witchcraft has evolved into a multi-billion dollar industry and carries an impressive thriving presence on the Internet.

This book is for the curious beginner who would like to learn how to practice rituals and craft their own spells. Learning how to successfully perform magic spells will bring positive experiences into your life, open your mind to possibilities you have never dreamed, and enhance the lives of those you love. All you need is the proper education and knowledge of spell crafting to get started.

More than ten years ago, after a bad break-up with my partner and losing my job, I felt as if my life was spiralling out of control. I wanted to get back on a spiritually positive path and regain my self-worth. I was introduced to magic by a close friend. I learned some basic magical spells and rituals as a way to distract myself from my woes. I never imagined that I would not only regain control over my emotions, but also the power to be the captain of my own ship and the master of my destiny. Unlike Humpty Dumpty, I was put back together again.

The type of people known as witches today is ever-changing. Even if the wizards and witches of fantasy and fairy tales aren't real, the people they are based on are! Many today refer to the over one million members of the pagan movement as witches. Believe it or not, most people who refer to themselves as witches don't announce it by wearing gothic clothes, tattoos, and body piercings. Most look just like the average joe—a single mom taking her kid to soccer practice, the mailman, a computer technician, and others with utterly innocuous appearances. One of my best friends, who played a big part in my introduction to witchcraft, worked as a microbiologist for the National Institute of Health when we first met. She would drive to work in her PT Cruiser, dressed in khakis and her lab coat, and wore her hair in a short red shag. The scientists she consulted with daily had no idea she regularly practiced moonlight rituals in her backyard only five miles away.

The point is, witches are far from the stereotype of people interested in devil worship, but in some ways, Hollywood does get it right. We do gather in circles, conduct moon rituals, use the magical energies of candles, crystals, and herbs. I use my wand to guide my spiritual energy in the right direction. We chant, connect with the Elements, and honor Mother Earth. This book will teach you how to let go of the some-times-monotonous material world and enter into a heightened state of awareness, one that will allow you practice powerful magic!

I

MODERN WITCHCRAFT

Witchcraft is a broad term for the belief and practice of magic. It can be found in various cultures across history and means something slightly different to every group. Social scientists define witches as people who practice magic from their inner-being, intentions, and intuitions. Basically, your higher self.

Throughout history, people of all cultures blamed witchcraft for any events or happenings that couldn't be predicted or explained, such as hunger, disease, mental illness, physical deformities, accidental death, and even societal problems. The people who were accused of causing these events were usually minorities or some type of social outcast. In general, people who didn't conform to the prevailing religion of their culture were seen as witches or sorcerers. Individuals who were accused of witchcraft tended to reflect the societal and political agendas of that period in time.

MISCONCEPTIONS ABOUT BEING A WITCH

Misconception #1: Witches are imaginary

Witches are real! They're just regular people who happen to practice magic. Practicing magic is about directing and raising your energy to manifest your intentions. The best way to know if you want to practice magic is to first clear up any misconceptions you may have about witches and witchcraft. Being a witch is about knowing yourself, learning how to empower yourself, and then putting that power into action.

Misconception #2: Being a witch requires tons of training

Another misconception you may have about witches is that it takes loads of training from established witches before you can start casting spells. Every time you make a wish and blow out a birthday candle, you are practicing magic. Don't get me wrong, doing your homework and a bit of research is always a good idea.

You don't need years of training from established witches before you cast your first spell. Putting pen to paper and writing a spell doesn't require belonging to a coven, waiting for a full moon, or dangling around some chicken's feet. Casting a spell only requires setting an intention and then performing a ritual to fulfill it, be that mediating, lighting a sage bundle, or taking a lavender scented bath. Once you understand what it means to direct your energy into an intention, you are on your way. I use all of those helpful hints every time I want to improve my creative writing. It works!

For example, let's say you want to start each day filled with more self-love. Write your intention down on paper affirming your gratitude, and then perform a ritual by lighting a candle. The ritual is reading out loud your affirmation while lighting a candle. Making a mantra or a chant (repeating your words) on your own is practicing magic. That is one example out of the many ways you can direct your energy into manifesting a desire. Have you ever noticed when someone walks towards you really fast, you can feel it? It's uncomfortable. You are feeling their vibration, their energy. It's invisible but you can feel it as much as you can feel rain. Casting a spell is harnessing your unseen vibrational energy into the right direction to lead you to your goal.

Misconception #3: Magic is expensive

Now that practicing magic has become popular and is no longer synonymous with evil, accessibility to knowledge, tools, and altar supplies are as easy to find as anything else you use on a daily basis. These days, using vegan, organic, and cruelty-free products are considered to be a practice in spirituality.

Be careful, though, because the witchcraft industry has just as much supply and demand as any other products in a store. You really don't have to spend a hundred bucks on goops and gadgets promising magic.

All you really need is yourself. Buy or pick up things you are drawn to. That can be a piece of driftwood or a special candle. Your intuition will tell you what you need. Later in the book there is a detailed description of the tools and materials that come in handy when casting spells. Certain items hold a charge that enhances the vibrational energies you direct into them. For example, I love my wand. It feels like an extension of my arm. I visualize and concentrate my wishes or intentions through my body and into my wand. Then I can point or wave that energy in the direction I want it to go. You've heard the expression *"Will it into existence."* Magic is just that!

Misconception #4: All witches are women

Witches come in all shapes, colors, genders, cultures, etc. It doesn't matter who you are or where you come from, you can be a witch. There is a rich history of women and witchcraft, partly because if a woman spoke her mind, she was called a witch, but truthfully, witchcraft is genderless.

Misconception #5: You have to come from an ancestry of witches

Some witches come from a long family history of witches and harnessing the energy of one's ancestors can be very powerful. We all have many ancestors, so summing the spirit of your ancestors, witches or not, is still a powerful form of magic.

Misconception #6: White witches are good and black witches are evil

Black witches should never be associated with black magic. That's just silly. I try to steer away from the terms "black magic" and "white magic." It has a racist undertone. Hoodoo is traditional African folk magic and was mistaken for being "bad" and thereby labeled "black magic." Honestly, magic isn't good or bad, it is simply a tool we use so we can interact on a deeper level with the Universe. Like anything else, there are those who are petty or jealous, who may act selfishly from time to time, and their magic can be used for hexes. In general, magic should never be used to cause harm. So, another *misconception* is believing hexes aren't real. They sure are!

Misconception #7: You must join a coven to be a witch

Covens are a group of witches who meet on a regular basis to perform rituals and magic together. Some covens are 13-membered traditional groups with an initiation process that is highly organized. Other covens are less structured and can be designed by you and a group of your witchy peers. Some people like the structure and responsibilities that come with belonging to a coven, and some witches prefer to "fly" solo. It is your decision to make, but by no means do you have to belong to a coven to practice witchcraft.

Kitchen Witch

Adding some tender loving care to the foods you prepare for yourself and loved ones is a form of magic. Preparing dishes with your own two hands and using herbs from your own garden infuses the dishes you make with magic. Using witchcraft in your culinary life can change the way you imagine, develop, prepare, and enjoy your meals. Kitchen witches perform the most basic levels of magic. The more you develop your magical skills, the more of a magical repertoire you have to draw from on a daily basis.

Taking the time to put together some basic ingredients for your meals is a magical opportunity to see your spells manifest in the most loving and special way. You can infuse every meal with your will and your intention. Cooking becomes a ritual that lends sacredness to each meal, and leaves you wanting to savor your magic with your family rather than just scarfing down a meal on your way out of the door to get to work.

Using magical instruments, such as cauldrons, crystals, and candles, creates a magically inspired ambiance. Keeping your kitchen sacred is a most important characteristic of being a kitchen witch. Writing your recipes in your Kitchen Book of Shadows, learning how to infuse your magic in the way you stir your foods in either a widdershins (counterclockwise) or a deosil (clockwise) direction is like adding fairy dust to your recipes.

I have a separate altar in my kitchen. Your stove top is equivalent to yesterday's fireplaces, and it's where most magical rituals for dining are done. I keep my herbs in jars I have decorated and chanted over. What I love most is my herb garden on the windowsill. Fresh ingredients are essential to the kitchen witch.

Green Witch

Green witches use the power of natural magic and healing through essential oils, plants, flowers, and herbs. They embrace all of the powers nature has to offer, and draw their energy from Mother Earth and the Universe. Green witches rely on natural materials such as crystals and stones to align with the land they live off. They call on nature to guide them and show great respect for all living beings. Making potions and oils from plants, flowers, and herbs is the way of the Green witch. Green witches believe working with crystals, stones, soils, and even twigs can help to find inner peace, balance, and unblock the chakras.

If you are drawn to natural things, feel you have a gift for soothing and healing, and enjoy taking care of herbs, plants, and gardens, you could be a green witch.

Hedge Witch

Hedge witches tend to practice solo. They don't adhere to any strict spiritual, religious, or otherwise dogmatic principles. They primarily focus their magic on creating healing remedies, by working herbs, the elements, crafts, and nature. They like to keep things basic and simple, and don't get involved with fussy rituals. They are essentially minimalists. If you want to craft your own brand of magic and are drawn to privacy, then you may want to consider being a hedge witch.

Crystal Witch

Crystal witches connect deeply to the vibrational powers of crystals, stones, rocks, and gems. They perform crystal magic to amplify, manifest, and attract energy. If you feel energies, see auras, enjoy creating crystal grids, and love shiny things, then you might be drawn to crystal witchery.

I was first attracted to crystals as a young child when my mom took me shopping at a small shop. I felt pulled towards a particular crystal and begged my mother to buy it. I then collected several more as I grew up, long before I knew anything about magic. Today, I believe crystals were my "gateway drug" into magic and have come to realize that crystals are like that for many people. Most who believe in the healing powers of crystals have yet come to realize they are practicing magic.

Each crystal has its own unique vibrational energy. These vibrations can bring balance and healing and can help you to direct your intentions into the universe according to your will. If you are drawn to crystals and enjoy learning about their magical uses and properties, you can become a Crystal Witch.

Eclectic Witch

A little piece of this type of witchcraft and a little bit of that type of witchcraft describes the eclectic witch. Eclectic witches tend to cherry-pick whatever rituals, beliefs, ideas, or practices that feel good or natural to them at the moment. Practicing witchcraft is a very unique and personal pursuit. If it's not your nature to be tied into one way of thinking or to any specific way of practicing, chances are you would gravitate to becoming an eclectic witch.

Eclectic witchcraft is sometimes thought of as modern witchcraft. Many solitary practitioners are eclectic witches. However, there are eclectic covens out there, too. Eclectic witches tend to find themselves mixing and matching traditions. They use a blend of practices and beliefs from a variety of pantheons and traditions. Some eclectic witches practice modified versions of traditional Gardnerian or Alexandrian Wicca, while still others entirely create their own set of practices and beliefs. Also, uninitiated practitioners often refer to themselves as eclectic or solitary because they are not using oathbound materials.

Gray Witch

Gray witches straddle the line between "white" and "dark" magic, using either one according to the situation they are handling. They will use hexes and curses accordingly. Most witches have ethical guidelines they follow, and outright choose to not go into any gray areas. Some witches use their magic to correct unfair circumstances and to seek justice by redirecting negative energies to where they believe it should have been in the first place. Gray witches are drawn to the darker side of magic because they believe they are fighting the evils in the world.

Cosmic Witch

Cosmic witches love to delve into astronomy and astrology. Stargazing is a favorite pastime for the cosmic witch. Their primary focus is lunar magic, the phases of the moon, and spells to protect against or amplify cosmic events. They are well versed on birth charts and star signs. Their practices are active, not passive, as they use their knowledge to manipulate vibrational energies, rather than telling you such and such is going to happen because you are a Sagitarrius. If you are drawn to the stars and the skies and like the complexities of the Universe, then you might be interested in becoming a cosmic witch.

Wiccans

Wicca is an organized form of religion. Wiccans worship two deities, the Moon Goddess and the Horned God who represent the feminine and masculine energies; the yin-yang of nature and the Universe.

The Goddess and God represent opposing forces of nature and creation. Wiccan covens follow initiations that symbolize rebirth, like resurrection in the Christian religion; initiates dedicate themselves to the goddesses and gods of their choosing. Wiccans can be solo witches through a self-dedication ceremony. Wiccans use magic and spells as a method of harnessing and redirecting natural energy to effect change. Magic is used as a tool that can be used by anyone with a little practice. Wiccan usually function through a set of ethical guidelines on how and why magic should be practiced.

II

THE TOOLS OF THE TRADE

There are many who may tell you that you must have a toolkit filled with magical items to cast your spells. Not true! Everything you need to practice magic is within you, except for those things you have yet to learn. Tools, however, are a great way to help you to focus your intentions and your energies for your magical practice. They are a great deal of fun, and for me they are inspiring. Just about anything you see around you can be a magical tool. A twig from a tree, salt from your pantry, a few coins from your wallet, you name it. Once filled with your intentions, everyday items can become powerful instruments of magic. I made a wand out of a small branch I found in my backyard. I carved it and decorated it myself, giving it a very special place in my heart.

The list of materials and tools for a beginner practicing witchcraft is a long one. If you were to Google:

Witchcraft, tools of the trade, you would find tarot cards, pentacles, wands, athames, cauldrons, bells, crystals, candles, essential oils, and books upon books of herbal remedies, and the list goes on. Just know that you are the most important tool, and your intuition will guide you toward what you need and the basics for newbie witches is never exhaustive. You first have to decide which path you're going to take.

Personal uniqueness is why witchcraft is so special! Every witch's path is different and uniquely personal. I have been blessed to befriend all types of witches. From traditional witches to eclectic witches, and from kitchen witches to green witches to hedge witches, I have friends who are deeply involved in deity and ancestral worship, and some who are devoted to science and atheism. So, grab a writing pad, a cup of your favorite tea, find a quiet place to sit, and write down the things that are most important to you. Then, prioritize them.

When you're finished with your list, look it over as a whole picture and read what in its entirety is telling you. Next, include in your list the subjects you're drawn to the most. Listen to your intuition. Include a psychological profile of interesting topics, such as self-love, ancestor veneration, shadow working, or cultural practices. Once you have revised your list to include all of those concepts, you have started the beginning of your guided path and to what will be your craft!

The tools you use directly relate to the type of craft you want to practice and who you are as a practitioner. You can decide you want all the tools, a few, or none at all. I've seen the whole spectrum of practitioners where tools are concerned. Here I will refer you back to Tip #1. Use your list of areas to decide what tools you want, if tools are suggested. Tools come in all shapes and sizes and carry a wide range of price tags from extremely expensive to free. If you ask me, the best tools are the ones you acquire yourself through nature. The best wand I've got is from an ash branch that I took home and carved myself.

ALTARS AND SHRINES

Altars and shrines are sacred places for rituals and spell casting. They can be designed or constructed anywhere you are drawn to setting one up. While most witches place traditional tools on their altars and shrines, you can use whatever your intuition tells you to, and whatever can fit your budget. Make sure you have all the items you need prior to casting your spells or starting a ritual. Altars are as easy to make as placing a cloth on a small table. If you are going to be practicing magic outdoors, you can use an old tree stump, a flat rock, or the top of your favorite cooler.

If your living space is on the smaller side, using the top of your dresser or nightstand will suit your needs. You can make your altar portable, if you want it to be private. You can then pack it up, put it in a safe place, and set it back up when you need it. You can use the bag you keep your altar materials in as your altar cloth. You can have altars for the seasons or permanent year-round altars. I like to make little altars in almost every room in my house: I have one in my kitchen, one next to my computer, and one in my bedroom. Some of my witch friends have altars to honor their ancestors with photos, heirlooms, and some even have urns of their deceased family members or pets.

I will always remember the first natural altar I saw. It had three seashells, a piece of bamboo, a few river rocks, and other really cool items that honored each of the elements. Your altar is as personal as your spiritual journey, so use it as a sacred place that holds things dearest to your heart.

When setting up your altar, you want to make sure your magical tools make your altar functional. You'll want to include your wand, and anthem, and your Book of Shadows to start. It must serve the purpose of manifesting your intentions. Here are some of the most common items found on witches' altars to represent the four classical elements and the four cardinal directions:

- A small container of soil or sand to align with the element Earth placed in the northern aspect of your altar.
- Some incense or essential oils to represent the element Air placed in the most eastern aspect of your altar.
- A candle to represent the element Fire placed in the most southern aspect of your altar.
- A tiny cup of spring water or moon-blessed water to represent the element Water placed in the western part of your altar.

CLEANSING AND CHARGING YOUR TOOLS

There are various methods for charging and cleaning your magical items. I always start with a wonderful sage smudging ritual. Sage cleansing is different from charging. Sage is an air purifier. You run your item through the smoke and then follow it with charging.

Here's how to charge an item:

1. Choose an item. The item you choose depends on what you want manifested through it. You may have a certain tool such as a crystal or a wand. Maybe you want to charge your car keys or your keyboard each morning, or the pens and pencils you use for your Book of Shadows. The list of items you can charge is endless.

2. Pick a charging method.

    a. I love to charge my items under a full moon and fill them up with lunar energy. The sun works, too. The sun and moon charge and cleanse at the same time. Simply place your items under the moonlight. Full and new moons are the strongest. Focus your intent for a few moments and let them charge.

    b. Charge with crystals. You can charge your crystals under the moon or various other methods, and they will then be able to transfer that charge to other objects. All you must do is have the crystal and the other items touch each other.

3. Visualizing: Rub your hands together until they feel tingly and warm. With your eyes closed, rub your hands together one more time. Slowly move your hands apart, being careful not to fling them apart, or you'll have to start over. Feel the energy bubbling up between your hands. It will feel stretchy and bouncy. Visualize the bubble, while you focus your intent into the item. Chant or speak aloud your intention. Visualize yourself pushing your intention into the bubble, and picture it changing color based on that intention: green for money, gold for abundance, silver for protection, pink for friendship, etc.

4. Earth Charging: Put the object in a potted plant overnight or in your outdoor garden.

5. Lunar Charging: Best done on new and full moons. Place your object in a windowsill or outside where it can be seen with your naked eye to reflect the moonlight. I also put glass containers (many of them) filled with spring water or tap water to make Moon Blessed Water. Then I use the water to water my plants, charge my altar items, feed my pets, add to my aroma diffuser, and in my morning coffee. You get the idea!

Carvings from as far back as the Stone Age portray wand-type images as powerful objects. In present day Great Britain, government officials keep on their person the "wand of office" to represent their power. Your witch's wand is used to channel and direct your magical intentions to influence your desired outcomes rather than for commands. Wands are aligned with both elements Air and Fire, and are used in rituals, for casting circles, and for crafting spells. Similar to the Athame, the wand is considered a masculine tool because of its phallic symbolism.

The witch's wand works as an extension of the person wielding its powers. It corresponds with the element Air and is therefore associated with communication, logic, and intellect. You can make a wand with anything you feel drawn to. Mine is made of beechwood and has a clear quartz crystal ball attached to the tip. I use it for so many things. I use it to carve sigils, words, and symbols into my candles. I charge my crystals with it. I also keep it charged on a daily basis. I either stick it in a potted plant for Earth charging, or I smudge it with burning sage. I have put it on the roof of my car during a full moon for lunar charging and lunar magic. I have also kept it in my lavender plant overnight and then it carries a lavender aroma with it throughout the day. I keep it on my keyboard when I'm working for a bit of technomancy. Willow wands have historically been used for healing magic.

BOOK OF SHADOWS

The Book of Shadows, or BOS, is a place for you to keep information that you will need in your magical practices. I prefer to handwrite my spells and recipes with a fountain pen, but you can use whatever your intuition wants, even if it is a virtual BOS. I like writing in my BOS with my own hand because I can feel my intentions transferring into content. Whatever works best for you, but keep in mind that your BOS is a sacred tool, and as such it should be consecrated along with the rest of the tools in your magical toolkit.

I can't possibly stress to you that things can seem very overwhelming to a new witch. But, if you zero in on one area and take one step at a time, it will seem much less daunting, that is if you make the commitment to recording everything. If you keep good records about what you have done, mistakes you think you may have made, and your feelings during each step of the journey, you will have great ideas about what works, and which places could use a bit of refinement.

You can keep smaller binders called grimoires, which are like having a mini-Book of Shadows for things like a kitchen grimoire, and garden grimoire, spiritual bathing grimoire, and so on. One of the biggest challenges facing beginner grimoire makers is the blank page. There it is, that pristine, white page staring up at you, begging the question, "And?" Or perhaps you can't even decide whether to start a Book of Shadows or a grimoire first.

As with your BOS, there are decisions to make

about how to organize your grimoire, how it should be organized, what medium you want to use, and what you want your finished grimoire to represent. I have coached many a newbie who puts off starting their grimoire because they want to launch themselves right into spell work. Some beginners thought they could just look up or buy a spell off of the internet and, "poof," magic happens. Oops, sorry, it doesn't quite work like that. Even beginners' luck needs to have the right ingredients, even if they came along by accident. I started out with my first Book of Shadows, and then found out I had about ten grimoires contained in it.

The biggest challenge you may face when putting together your Book of Shadows is organization. If you have really good organizational skills, you can create a table of contents. I use a three-ring binder so I can move things around and add things to different sections as I go along. Remember, witchery is a progressive technique. The more I learn, the more I realize I know very little.

If you come across a spell, ritual, or recipe that is not originally yours, make sure to reference your source. It is respectful and allows you the opportunity to share information with your friends about what you have learned and where you have been finding such powerful magic.

What to include in your Book of Shadows

1. If you have a certain tradition or belong to a coven, magic does have some rules. Write

them down and keep them in the front of your Book of Shadows to remind you of your Witch's Code of Ethics. If you are a Solitary witch, write down your own code of ethics.

2. A dedication is optional, but I feel really good about it. You can dedicate your BOS to anyone, any deity, or even an Element if you choose. I have a Book of Shadows I dedicated to Mother Moon. It says, "I, Bridget, dedicate this Book of Shadows to the Mother Moon," on this date, and I put the date I started that BOS. I made an entire BOS on just lunar magic.

3. Correspondence Charts, Symbols, and Tools: Knowing which colors, crystals, shapes, herbs, lunar phases, elements, along with their magical properties, is probably the most important information a Witch needs to have close by. It's a real pain in the neck to have to Google for correspondences several times a day. You might not yet be practicing spells several times a day, but you are practicing magic every time you are trying to make something happen in your life. (**Note: I also put down which herbs are okay to consume, because some are good for their aroma, some for their health benefits, and some to ward off evil.)

4. Witch's holidays: Esbats, Sabbats, and other pagan holidays if that is your tradition have a

history of rites carried out on those special days. It's nice to have a reference guide that you wrote yourself, so you can tailor it to the things you most enjoy. I have things like How to Cast a Circle and Drawing Down the Moon also in my BOS.

5. And, of course, your spells!

ATHAMES

Athames are used to channel energy. Often, witch's use athames to cast a circle or to call upon the powers of the elements. I use mine for scribing my intentions in the soil of my herbs, in my candle rituals, and for the aesthetics of my altar. The athame corresponds with the Element Fire. You can make your own double-edged dagger or athame or pick one up at your local mystical shop. You can use your athame in place of your wand whenever you feel the urge.

WITCH'S BROOM OR BESOM

The witch's besom or broom is quite literally used for sweeping your sacred space before a ceremony or ritual. It physically and metaphorically sweeps away any unwanted spirits and negative energy that may have gathered since you last cleansed your space. The besom corresponds with the Element Water, so it functions as a purifier. One of my friends has a collection of handmade besomes from countries all around the world. I put a few drops of pine essential oil on mine during the winter months and cinnamon or tea tree oil during the fall. Summer time I use lemon essential oils on my besom, so all year round it functions as aromatherapy and as a space cleanser. I sweep away negative energy right out the door, and then off of the sidewalk near the door. Traditional witch's brooms were made from willow wands with a birch twig bundle bound around the end.

People are increasingly becoming fascinated with the ancient Celtic ritual of handfasting. During wedding ceremonies or unification ceremonies, the couple's hands are tied together. This ceremony is also referred to as "jumping the broom." During the times of slavery, the custom of jumping the broom was part of wedding ceremonies in the American South, because the couples had very little in their lives.

WITCH'S BELL

In the world of witchcraft, ringing bells initiate a change in the essence of the Universe. Wind chimes tell us when the weather is changing. The black cat, who is otherwise silent, announces their presence. The doorbell tells us we have a visitor. Clock bells mark the changing of time.

While bells do notify us of physical changes, their sounds indicate an energetic change, as well. You can feel their energy when you think about Santa ringing the bell for the Salvation Army, or when we need to chase away or banish an unwanted spirit. For protection, bells can guard an entrance to your home. The

Ancient Romans used wind chimes, called tintinnabulum, on the temple gates to ward off evil.

We use bells in our witchy workings to seal in the magic of a spell. It's a finishing bell that shifts the intent into manifestations. I keep a small dinner bell on my altar and seal all of my spells with a ding-aling-aling. You can attune your personal unique energy to a certain pitch of a bell. The vibration and sound can reset any negative or errant energy and help you to get back on your feet, or back to your personal frequency. When I seal my spells with the ringing of a bell, I can feel the ringing inside of me. That is because the bell toll is a form of vibrational energy. Everything in the universe has an energy vibration, so bells have been resonating with humans for millennia. Ancient Grecians rang cymbals (sistra) to ward off disease and to promote fertility, and present-day energy practitioners use tonal healing to align and unblock chakras.

The ringing of a bell can invoke the spirits of the elements, also known as Calling the Quarters. Funeral bells have long been associated with the spirits of the dead. Funeral bells are rung traditionally around the world.

CRYSTALS

Crystals are powerful agents used for healing, love, money, and much more. They bring forth positive and bountiful vibrations that when directed by your intention can flow through the body and take toxic or negative energy away. Each crystal has its one specific vibration and frequency that comes from what they are made from on a molecular level. The molecules in a crystal interact with each other and form vibrations. They function like a magnet for negativism, attach their vibrations to it, and draw it away. Because they are created by nature, they harness the energies of the moon, the oceans, the sun, the earth, and the wind and then use those energies for lifting our moods, healing our bodies, minds, and soul, and improving our overall health and wellness.

The most important aspect of working with gems and crystals is to make a personal connection with each one of them. Learn how to recognize and feel the energy of the crystal. That is how to establish a connection and make it stronger.

THE MEANING OF THE SHAPES OF CRYSTALS

Crystals come in different colors, like rose, amethyst or aquamarine, and are used for varying purposes, such as protection, attraction, health and wellness, sleep improvement, etc. They are also formed into many differing shapes. The crystalline structure doesn't affect the type of energy it puts out; the shape of the crystal does, however, affect the way you receive its energy. The shape of your crystal can help to ramp up your experience and your purpose. So, choosing the shape of a crystal should complement your intention and magnify and enhance your transformation.

Here are some of the crystal shapes and their magical influences:

1. Cubes

If you are looking for a great grounding gem, a cube-shaped crystal is the way to go. Cupping a cube-shaped crystal in your hands connects you to the Element Earth's vibrational energies. They are also perfect for protecting your home or office by placing one in each of the corners in your home, car, or office.

2. Pyramids

The base of pyramid-shaped crystals serves as an intention's anchor. It's apex structure points your intentions out into the universe. Pyramid crystals are powerful ways to manifest your intention.

3. Spheres

Sphere-shaped crystals represent being part of the greater good and remind you that all the energies in the environment surrounding you are interconnected. The crystals' sphere-shape provides you with a Zen vibe, so they function beautifully for meditation.

4. Tumbled Crystals

These smooth and small crystals are thought to be the magical stepping stones into the universe's vibrational energies. Just because they are small doesn't make them any less powerful. They make great travel companions, so you can physically carry your magic while on the go. Having a few in your desk drawer, glove compartment, or in your pocket will keep your energy boosted as you go about your day.

5. Crystal points

Crystal points have sharp tips that keep your mind sharp, too. It is the go-to crystal when you need to be laser-focused on a task at hand. I write my intention down on a small square of paper, and in a pyramid fashion, I set the crystal point on top. The crystal points your intention powerfully out into the universe and into your personal environment.

6. Crystal hearts

Crystals that are heart-shaped have been cut and polished this way. They do not naturally occur, but they still promote powerful love energy. I love giving these little hearts as gifts to my friends. Several of my friends keep the hearts I have given them throughout the workday, and have told me they make a huge difference in their energy level while working.

7. Crystal Clusters

Crystals clustered together are a beautiful sight to see! They sparkle and hold mystical vibrations in their natural form. Place a crystal cluster on the entrance way to your home and in the center of a boardroom table to promote open-mindedness and community. I keep one on the dining table at home, making it always a topic for discussion, even though I have been building one each evening for years.

WHAT IS A CRYSTAL GRID?

A crystal grid is an amazingly powerful instrument of energy to manifest your intentions and to heal your body, mind, and spirit. Arranging your crystals according to your intuition is making a crystal grid. Simply placing them down on your altar with consideration or with infusing your intention is not considered a grid. The power of the grid is created by the union of vibrational energies derived from the crystals. Using a crystal grid combines the powers of the crystals into the pattern you have created; it multiples their energies.

When I was 9 or 10 years old, my mother took me to a very cluttered antique shop, well hidden somewhere between my house and Timbuktu. I say Timbuktu because at the age of 9, anything more than 15 minutes in the car seemed like days. I didn't mind going to antique shops, because there were always interesting items, but none that I really ever deeply felt a need to take home with me. This specific trip to the store was anything but ordinary. My mother loved unique knick-knacks with hidden meanings, but she wasn't a hoarder. I saw the glass case by the cash register and felt the most amazing pull towards this crystal. In the corner of the case were "the round ones." They were small spheres of crystal quartz, and believe it or not, I felt compelled to grab one. You will too! We will cover the color meanings of crystals and candles in the same section since they correspond with one another. So, let's talk about candles.

CANDLES

It's obvious that fire is energy, therefore, candles represent energy. It is the transformation of energy that takes place when you light a candle. An unlit candle holds energy in a dormant state. When you light it, the energy is released through the flame, and affected by the air. I put an intention each morning, pick a candle that is calling my name, light it, and let it send that intention out into the universe all day long while I am working. It is an amazing feeling. I can glance over at it from time to time and see that it is still working. I imagine my intention flowing out of the flame and picture the Universe embracing it. Simply fascinating! It is always about your intention. Before I learned about magic, a candle was just a candle. I didn't know it was capable of such a powerful influence on the way my day went. Fire transforms everything. When we make a meal, fire transforms our ingredients from raw to cooked. Once you understand how to apply your influence to fire, you can then shape the transformation process.

Primarily, candles correspond with the Element Fire. The reason candles are so magically potent is because they rely on all the elements working together. The candle's base symbolizes the Earth

Element and is therefore grounding. The melting wax symbolizes the Element Water that runs and reshapes the form of things. The flame depends on the Element Air to keep burning and dancing, as oxygen must be present for a candle to burn. Burning a candle changes the atmosphere and makes us more aware of the presence of energies normally unseen. When I gaze at a flickering flame, I am able to meditate effortlessly. It takes you to a place of calmness and understanding.

While fire is the key element of energy in practicing candle magic, the color, the shape, and whatever you carve into the candle customizes your spells to fit your intention.

COLOR CORRESPONDENCES

When choosing your candle or a crystal for your magical practices, be mindful of its color. Colors correspond with specific elements and characteristics. Choosing the color aligned with your intention will increase the strength of your spell. Here are some basic correspondences:

- *Green* corresponds with nature and fertility, as well as money and good fortune.
- *Red* corresponds with power and passion, as well as vitality and courage.
- *Pink* corresponds with friendship and romance, as well as compassion and innocence.

- *Yellow* corresponds with success and happiness, as well as travel and imagination.
- *Blue* corresponds with truth and communication, as well as fidelity and patience.
- *Orange* corresponds with creativity and joy, as well as ambition and justice.
- *Purple* corresponds with wisdom and spiritual power, as well as warding off evil.
- *Silver* corresponds with intuition and dreams.
- *White* corresponds with purity and cleansing, as well as peacefulness and balance.
- *Black* corresponds with grounding and learning, as well as protection and banishment.

HERBS

Historically, there was no difference between medicine and magic. While we now know that medicine works on our physical bodies, magic works on our spiritual bodies. Herbal magic is practical magic! Many of the herbs in your pantry can be homegrown or easily purchased from local stores, farmer's markets, and shops. Of course, all self-respecting witches practicing herbal magic own a mortar and pestle, a recipe Book of Shadows, and the appropriate bottles and jars.

In my Herbal Book of Shadows, I enjoy writing down the folklore, traditions, and tales about my herbs. To start your own collection, gather a few bottles, and some berries, leaves, bark, and seeds. That is all that is necessary to concoct recipes powerful enough to enhance your spells.

When speaking of herbal magic, we're not talking about just the herb, we are also referring to its roots and its flowers. Witches honor all things natural and wild, so using gifts provided by Mother Earth is only fitting. It's easy to understand why herbs are believed to be the oldest known magical instruments.

THE TWO RULES OF HERBAL MAGIC

1. The oils in herbs and spices are where all of the flavor is. They can go bad or dissipate after a while, so keep your spices whole and grind them yourself as needed. You can purchase the following pre-ground: turmeric, garlic, sumac, and cinnamon. Throw away old spices.
2. At first, use recipes that have been passed down or are tried and true. With a little experimentation, you will learn in what ratios and how to combine your herbs. After creating some blends from recipes written by herbalists, start getting creative with your herbal blends, and creating your own recipes will become second nature.

Here are a few of the herbs in my pantry and their magical correspondences:

- **Allspice**: Money, positivity, luck, uplifting mood, increases energy, and determination.
- **Basil**: Love spells, protection rituals and spells, prosperity spells, hedge riding (astral travel), purification, peace, and banishment.
- **Black Pepper**: Protection, exorcism, jealousy, negativity, strength, confidence, and gossip.
- **Cayenne**: Spiritual connection, strengthens the magical powers of other herbs, purification of water and home, rids the home of negative energy, removes obstacles, and helps you reach your goals.
- **Cinnamon**: Esotericism, white magic, healing, protection, love, success, power, and sexual desire.
- **Cloves**: Enhances spiritual vibrations, purification, prosperity, wards off negative and hostile forces, clarity, empathy, healing, and memory.
- **Cumin**: Fidelity, repels evil, love, peace, exorcism, passion, aphrodisiac, and protection against thieves.
- **Dill**: Lust, protection, money, luck, love, warding off dark forces, blessing your house, keeping you informed about the difference between superstition and magic, and attraction.

- **Echinacea**: Money, offerings, protection, power, exorcism, added strength for spells and charms, fertility, healing, clairvoyant and psychic abilities.
- **Fennel**: Sexual virility, protection, purification, healing, courage, vitality, increase the length of incarnation, and ward off evil.
- **Ginseng**: Lust, beauty, love, money, wishes, healing, protection, sexual potency, health and wellness.
- **Saffron**: Happiness, strength, healing, love spells, lust, raising the power of wind, increasing psychic awareness, controlling the weather, and aphrodisiac.

HERBAL SACHET MAGIC

Herbalism has been part of the magical world since the beginning. Herbs are delicious, make wonderful potions, and tucked away into a sachet, the aroma will let you place a bit of your garden in any of the places you need cleansing, charging, or simply want to enjoy their fragrance. Make sure you choose a breathable fabric, such as hemp, burlap, or tea bag mesh for your sachets.

I keep a lavender sachet in my lingerie drawer, a mint sachet in the glove compartment of my car and use them in my clothes dryer to allow their scent to linger on my body throughout the day. You don't have to know how to sew, either. There are mesh bags out there to purchase, and pre-made sachets, too. Remember you are making magic, so making your own sachets infused with your intention is walking the walk of a witch. I make a lot of them around the holidays because they make such beautiful gifts. My friends tell me they are very special because not only are they handmade, they're like a bundled-up blessing that spreads love wherever they are placed.

The magic in putting together a sachet is using equal parts herbs and intuition. When you are choosing which herbs, flowers, or roots, pick those you are drawn to and that align with your intent. Your intuition is that gut feeling you have about whether something is wrong or right. There is no logic behind the feeling, it is just that: a gut feeling.

You can pay attention to your intuition. Maybe it is insisting that an item or ingredient isn't the right one for your intention. Herbs that work magic for me may not correspond with the wishes of the person I am gifting it to. Even if they weren't in need of its magical intentions, you can't go wrong giving a sachet as a gift. I put some TLC in all of my sachet gifts, because everyone can use a little TLC.

It is important to study your herb garden, so you know when the best time is for harvesting and drying to best preserve their fragrance. Here are the steps for you to learn how handcraft your own sachets, another fantastic perk of being a witch:

MATERIALS

Breathable fabric
Ribbon
Small bowl or Mortar & Pestle
Herbs of your choice, dried or fresh
Aromatic flower petals or dried flowers of your choice
Essential oils

STEPS

1. Determine what size you would like your sachet to be. I cut my fabric into 4 X 7-inch squares. You can get out the sewing machine and sew your squares together leaving the top open for stuffing or cut your squares bigger and then just bundle up your ingredients and tie the top of the pouch closed.
2. Gather enough herbs to blend together to fill your sachet.
3. While blending your herbs, keep in mind your intention. For example, if it is money, visualize the word "PAID" stamped on your bills. Chant: *Money Grows, Money Shines, Now More Money is mine! As it is and should be.*
4. Add ten drops of essential oils that match your herbal blend.
5. Stuff your sachet bags with the blended herb-oil mixture.

6. Tie the ends closed with string, ribbon, or you can glue them closed.
7. ENJOY!

Moth deterrent sachets

Ingredients: lavender, thyme, rosemary, and dried lemon peels. Fresh rosemary has a stronger aroma than dried rosemary, so growing some indoors allows you to freshen up your sachets year-round. If you are going to refresh your sachet, tie them shut instead of gluing them. As witches, we take coming unglued seriously!

ESSENTIAL OILS

Oils have been used ceremoniously in rituals for thousands of years. Back then, oils were made by heating fat into an oil, and then adding herbs or flowers to the oil. The essential oil industry is huge, but a lot of them are synthetic and only a fraction of the cost. For an oil to be essential, it has to be derived from a plant. When it comes to using oils for your magical practices, authentic essential oils are the way to go.

For rituals, you can dress your candles for use in spells. This is double magic: the superpowers of the essential oils fuse with the symbolism created by the flame, color, and shape of the candle. Essential oils have been used since ancient times to anoint the body. Be careful you are not using any oils that may be an irritant, such as clove and frankincense. Anointing Oils applied to the body are charged with your intent;

Energy Oil, Courage Oil, Money Oil, Confidence Oil, to name a few.

You can also use anointing oils on your crystals, amulets, talismans and other charms. This is a great way to turn a simple item into a talisman of magical power and energy.

MAGICAL PROPERTIES OF ESSENTIAL OILS

Essential oils can be added to lotions, ointments, cosmetics; turned into a vapor for your diffusers and aromatherapy; added to your bath water; or dry evaporated on a piece of cloth or fabric, functioning like a sachet.

- Peppermint: Energy, money
- Cedar: Protection, prosperity, purify
- Cinnamon: Power, protection, love
- Chamomile: Confidence, joy, growth
- Jasmine: Calming, love, dreams
- Lemon: Renewal, energy, cleansing, purify
- Orange: Success, confidence, sun magic
- Rose: Intuition, love, romance, beauty, protection
- Lavender: Anxiety reducer, cleanse, love
- Tea Tree: Angels, healing, money, protection
- Sandalwood: Spirits, love, peace

Instructions for Making your Own Oil Blends

1. Before you start, determine your intent. If it

is money, love, or health, you need to know what spells or rituals you want to manifest.

2. ⅛ Cup Base oil: Safflower, Grapeseed, Jojoba, Sunflower, and Almond
3. Drop your essential oil into the base oil with an eye dropper
4. Do not mix** Swirl the oils around in a clockwise direction blending them with the base.
5. Add to a dark-colored bottle.
6. Get creative with your labeling. I like to draw pictures of herbs or flowers. Make sure to date your labels, with an expiration date of 6 months.

BLESSING OIL

These oil blends are great for consecration, blessing, and anointing. They should be prepared in advance, so you have them standing by when you need them. Uses for blessing oils include blessing your magical tools, anointing a new baby, welcoming a new witch into a ritual circle.

Ingredients for Blessing Oil

1/8 Cup base oil of your choice
5 drops Sandalwood
2 drops Camphor
1 drop Orange
1 drop Patchouli

PROTECTION OIL

Oil blends for protection keep you safe from magical and psychic attacks. Use them in your car, home, property, on yourself and loved ones, and in the workplace. Protection oils always have mugwort and lavender.

Ingredients for Protection Oil

1/8 Cup base oil of your choice
4 drops Patchouli
3 drops Lavender
1 drop Mugwort

MONEY OIL

This oil blended up ahead of time is good for use in prosperity, abundance, money, and good fortune rituals. This is one of the most popular oils and is sold on the market. The ironic thing is that they can be expensive! When you make your own essential oils, there is a bit of 'you' in them.

Ingredients for Money Oil

⅛ Cup Grapeseed oil base
4 drops Cinnamon
4 drops Mint
2 drops Basil
2 drops Nutmeg

POWER ESSENTIAL OIL

This essential oil recipe will give all of your spells an extra boost. I always keep a vial of Power Oil on my altar. The scent of the eucalyptus immediately fuels my intent!

Ingredients for Power Oil

1/8 Cup base oil of your choice
Eucalyptus
Frankincense
Mandrake
10 drops Cinnamon

III

THE WHEEL OF THE YEAR

The ancient Celtics thought of time as cyclical: the birth and death of people, seasons come and go, all returns in some form or another, and the cycle naturally repeats itself. The Wheel of the Year celebrates eight Neo-Pagan holidays and celebrates the changing season with four solar festivals during the Winter Solstice, Spring Equinox, Summer Solstice, and the Fall Equinox. In modern days, the Wheel of the Year helps witches maintain balance in an uncertain and chaotic world.

The important days of the Wheel of the Year include:

Samhain (Sau-ihn)

1. Halloween
2. October 31st: Scorpio

3. Earth Event: Midpoint between the fall equinox and the winter solstice
4. Occasion: Celebrating the dead and cleaning and releasing. It commemorates the ending of the harvest season and a time for farmers to prepare their crops for the coming winter.

Yule

1. Christmas
2. December 20-25: Capricorn
3. Earth Event: Winter Solstice
4. Occasion: Lighting the sacred fire, fellowship, Song, and candle lighting

Imbolc (Im blk)

1. Candlemas
2. February 1-2: Aquarius
3. Earth Event: Midway between the Winter Solstice and the Spring Equinox
4. Occasion: Lunar Fire Festivals for celebrating the Earth Goddess's recovery after giving birth. Feasts and offerings are offered in her honor.

Ostara (ow staa ruh)

1. Easter
2. March 20-23: The first day of the Aries season

3. Earth Event: Spring Equinox
4. Occasion: Spring cleaning and planting seeds.

Beltane

1. May Day
2. April 30-May 1: Taurus season
3. Earth event: The midpoint between Spring Equinox and the Summer Solstice.
4. Occasion: Couples dance around a bonfire in celebration of fertility

Litha

1. Midsummer
2. June 20-22: Gemini reflects the fertile theme of Litha
3. Earth Event: Summer Solstice
4. Occasion: Gratitude for life and light. Honor the Sun God.

Lughnasadh (Lúnasa)

1. First Harvest
2. August: Leo is the proclaimed sign of the summertime
3. Earth Event: Halfway between the summer solstice and autumn equinox
4. Occasion: The first fruits given as an offering

to the deities, showing them they are
honoring hard work and that it pays off.

Mabon

1. Thanksgiving
2. September 20-23: Virgo
3. Earth Event: Autumnal equinox
4. Occasion: A time for finishing up projects
   and reaping what was sown, and then
   resting. After the long hard work of the
   harvest, it is a time for rest and recovery.

THE LUNAR CYCLE: HOW DIFFERENT PHASES OF THE MOON AFFECT US AND OUR MAGIC

I have been practicing lunar magic over the last ten years for its many gifts offered to all who ask and acknowledge her wisdom and power, and even to those who don't. When I was a small child, I sat on the sand and became entranced by the sheer size of that bright white ball just hanging up there in all her charm. I have always felt connected to the Mother Moon, and I am not alone. People have been worshiping the moon since the beginning of time, and in every culture. Sometimes, I feel sad when I see people mulling about their evenings, and sometimes during daylight, and there is a huge Supermoon putting on an exhibition larger than life, and some don't seem to notice. They fall into the old adage of not "stopping to smell the roses."

Moon gazing is a time for self-reflection. The lunar phases symbolize eternity, immortality, and the enlightenment of Mother nature which is sometimes referred to as the dark side. In her cycling phases, she is reflecting the phases of life and the inner-wisdoms of humankind.

If you have ever wondered how the Moon affects our behavior, moods, sleeping habits, temper, and so on, consider this: Since the moon is smaller than the sun and it is rotating, its gravitational pull is unequal, or it is stronger where it is closest to the Earth. That is why we have tides. Two-thirds of the world is water and the moon's powerful gravitational pull shifts all of that water around differently during each lunar phase; hence, the tides. Well, two-thirds of every living body is also water, so you can only imagine that the water in our bodies is affected by the shifting gravity of the moon and would therefore influence not only our behavior but the actions of all living things, from bugs to fish and right up to the King of the Beasts: Us.

THE MOON'S PHASES AND THEIR MAGICAL INFLUENCES:

1. **New Moon**: The dark moon is the beginning of the lunar phase, representing turning over a new leaf or new beginnings. Create a sacred lunar altar. It is a time to set your intentions, get going, plan for success, and

set goals for the future. It is the darkest night of the month and a good time for a candle lighting ceremony. In your BOS, jot down your intentions, your new moon list

2. **Crescent Moon**: Represents growth, the divine feminine, psychic visions, creation, and thriving.

3. **Waning Crescent Moon**: A time for cleansing rituals for you and your home. It represents doors closing, relationship endings, and the ending of spells previously cast. Its magic is used to banish evil or negative energies. It is called upon to break spells and have a fresh start.

4. **Waxing Crescent Moon:** Your strength and energy increase during this phase of the moon, as she is heading towards fullness. It's time to prepare for new projects.

5. **First Quarter Moon:** This is the time for spells to draw things in, such as success, money, good health, love, and for finding lost objects. It is a time for candle lighting, spiritual exercises with nature, spiritual bathing, and focusing on aligning and unblocking your chakras.

6. **Waning Gibbous Moon**: The word *waning* refers to the moon's diminishing light. Your energy levels may be diminishing and leaving you with feelings of gratitude. This phase is a time for sharing love, visiting old friends, and apologizing to anyone you may

have been grouchy with during the full moon.

7. **Waxing Gibbous Moon**: The illuminated side of the moon is increasing and headed towards fullness. So, it is a good time to practice patience, flexibility, and gratitude. It is a time for self-reflection. This phase presents an opportune time for consulting your runes and tarot cards.

8. **Full Moon:** Your cosmic life coach. The most spectacular, iconic, and notorious moment of the lunar cycle. It is literally and figuratively a clarity of the mind era. It is a time of great energy, which can turn the most introverted person into a social butterfly. Just be careful not to wear yourself out.

9. **Last Quarter Moon:** Represents spiritual healing, and a time for moving forward in life. It's a time for risk-taking and change. During this phase, examine what is and isn't working for you in your life and take corrective action. This is the "Now what?" phase.

DAYS OF THE WEEK

Now that you have learned about how to work your lunar magic, it's time to learn what you can do magically every day while waiting for the anticipated phases of the moon. There is so much to learn, but for the beginner witch, we're off to a great start! One of my favorite lessons in magic was learning how to work with the days of the week. Here is a brief overview of the magical aspects of the days of the week and their correspondences:

Monday: Corresponds with the element Water, the Zodiac sign Cancer, and the colors blue, grey, and white. It is the perfect day for channeling and enhancing your psychic abilities, dream work, intuition, emotions, fertility, and healing.

Tuesday: Corresponds with the element Fire, the zodiac signs of Aries and Scorpio, and the color orange. Tuesday magic is favorable for summoning strength, courage, passions, assertiveness, and boundary setting. Spells advocating justice and even baneful spells are most successful on Tuesday.

Wednesday: Corresponds with the elements Water and Air, the zodiac sign of Gemini, and the colors green, silver, and orange. Wednesday's magic is favorable for shadow work, personal development, communication, reconciliations, oration spells, and working on your relationships.

Thursday: Corresponds with the elements Air and Fire, the zodiac sign of Capricorn, and the colors brown and gray. Thursdays are the perfect day for spells of attraction, prosperity, luck, overcoming obstacles, legal matters, and personal success.

Friday: Corresponds with the element Earth, the zodiac sign of Taurus and the colors pink, red, and blue. Friday is associated with beauty, sex, love, and fertility, or how about a combination of all four? Glamor spells, sex magic, attract a new love interest, and conception are all wonderful working Friday spells.

Saturday: Corresponds with the elements Water and Earth, the zodiac sign of Sagittarius, and the colors of purple and black. Saturday is the best time to take out your black candles and work some banishing magic. Saturdays are associated with ending a partnership, relationship, employment, protection spells, swift karma, and justice.

Sunday: Corresponds with the element Fire, the zodiac sign of Leo, and the colors red, yellow, and orange. Spells for healing, protection, success, prosperity, fame, insight, empowerment, and for honoring your favorite deities. All of your spells are amplified on Sunday.

IV

SPELL CASTING

How magic works for many individuals is simply a way of connecting with your potential. You use your intuition and perceptions to examine your potential and then use an action to manifest that potential. Working with what is in plain sight yet is hidden to your senses requires you to learn the art of mindfully listening to the silence.

The first thing beginners need to learn is how your intuition functions. It's that little voice grumbling in the back of your head, maybe an image or a word cropping up in your mind telling you to turn left instead of right. To become connected to your intuition takes learning the importance of passing thoughts. Sometimes, it's revealed in your dreams, while meditating, via tarot, during a nature walk, or in shadow work.

Sometimes you may feel you should turn right instead of left. Acquiring the skill of identifying how your intuition presents itself and the difference from it feeling like a passing thought will help you practice ways in which you can pay attention to how and when your intuition manifests. Beginner witches need to learn how to trust their intuition and then comes learning how to fine tune it.

A good example is when you are having second thoughts. Maybe you don't have the best feeling about that expensive online outfit that looks so good on the screen, but your intuition tells you that what is in the picture is not what will come in the mail. You can wear crystals, light candles, and burn sage to help sharpen your abilities for listening to your intuition.

THE DOCTRINE OF SIGNATURES

The Doctrine of Signatures may be an age-old belief, but there is no denying its existence. In 1622 a German mystic, philosopher, and theologian named Jakob Boehme documented his findings regarding the resemblance between many plants and the exact body parts they are intended to treat!

Some plants were probably named so after-the-fact, being assigned names based on their health benefits, but that doesn't explain their resemblance to those very body parts. Historically, walnuts were used as a medicine for brain-related health issues. Today, walnut extracts, and walnuts contain essential fatty acids that improve memory and concentration. Furthermore, the meat of the walnut looks just like a brain in a skull! Amazing, isn't it? Lungwort has spotted leaves that resemble a diseased lung, and it is used for respiratory ailments. Lungwort is used in cough medicines!

From a mystical point of view, some believe that the Universe or Creator gave physical clues about the value she or he, or whatever gender your deity is, imbued to plants. All plants, trees, herbs, flowers, and other things which come out of the Earth are cosmic communications, books, and magic signs, to use by the immense mercy of the Universe or Creator.

CONTAMINATION AND MAGIC

You may have experienced feeling very uncomfortable in certain places or near certain things. Sometimes this happens when you have had a prior negative experience that you associate with the place. You're unlikely to be comfortable in the dentist's office. Sometimes we bring things into our environment that are still attached or linked to an evil spirit or some other type of unwanted spell or being.

Detecting signs of negative or evil energies in your home or on items is an essential skill to learn. There are varying signs of negative and evil signs that each one of us will face at some point in our lives. Knowing how to find and remove these spirits and energies at the start of your witchcraft journey will save you lots of trouble, provide you with better health, and protect your home and your loved ones. Your home should be a sanctuary, and items you pick up in stores, or that have been passed down through generations may have been handled or infused with unsavory energies.

Pay close attention to your feelings when you're home. Does each room have a welcoming and peaceful feeling? Do any rooms feel uncomfortable in a strange way? Is there one room that family members argue in the most? If you answered yes to any of those questions, now it is time for a cleansing. Our homes and the items in them tend to absorb energies from all who have lived in and with them. If you are feeling drained and confused, it is important to know that negative and evil energies cling to positive energies. If you are feeling positive and things start to suddenly change, try whipping out your sage bundle and smudging your area.

There is also a method known as the Glass of Water technique. All you need is some salt and water in a clean glass, and then put the glass in a dark corner of a room and leave it to sit undisturbed for 24 hours, without looking at it. If it looks the same, the room is free of evil spirits and negative energy, but if it is bubbling or has things floating around, chances are you need a cleansing.

Also, crystals can not only charge your home with energy, but they also work when you wear them as jewelry. Smoky quartz is a powerful stone for cleansing negative energy. If you sense something when you're wearing a certain item of clothing, put your unlit sage bundle in the same drawer, or wrap the item around a smoky quartz crystal. Clear quartz crystals are universal and work for clearing unwanted energies from homes, cars, and objects.

If you're in need of getting rid of something you

used for a banishing spell, like getting rid of your ex, once and for all. You probably want to get those objects that you used for the spell as far away as possible, like driving it an hour away from your house and burning it in the forest. Make sure all fires are completely put out before ever leaving them some place where a little bit of a breeze could start a wildfire.

WHAT IS A TALISMAN?

Magical thinking and superstition actually influence our brains more than you may believe. Consider that it doesn't matter how silly it may be, and even the most rational people feel it, but when you break a mirror it's a big, "Uh, oh, seven years of bad luck!" Fortunately, as a witch you can break that spell! You may think that is ridiculous, but it doesn't stop the ominous feeling that occurs if it happens. This is evidence of how our minds can be powerfully affected by everyday objects.

The same thing applies to objects we hold dear, that have sentimental value such as things passed down from our grandparents, or those items that represent an important event in your life or in history. Objects carry a great deal of psychic energy. A good example are the many religious relics such as the crucifix to the Catholics.

Using these same principles, we can create talismans to fit the needs of our intentions, beliefs, spellwork, and therefore use common objects as friends to work with in our craft. The word talismans coms from the Greek word *telesma* meaning *initiation*. They are physical items made of vegetable, mineral, or animal origin, that we can then charge with our intent. For instance, crystals correspond with astrological signs and the elements, and four-leaf clovers are associated with good luck. Other types of talismans include pentagrams and amulets.

Here are the steps for charging positive energy into a talisman of your own:

1. Select the physical base, such as a crystal that has a special meaning to you. It can be any natural object. It doesn't have to be costly, but solid enough for you to connect with its presence, touch, smell, weight, with a specified intention (e.g., dice are used by gamblers as talisman).

2. Transmit your positive intentions by spending five minutes a day for seven days to mediate your intention using the physical base. If you worship a deity or other spirit, visualize their energy infusing into your physical base, whichever base you have decided upon. I have a small jade crystal in the shape of an apple that I use as a good health talisman. This will connect your intent to the object, and the object therefore represents your intention, wishes, or positive emotions like love, luck, money, health, etc.

3. Charge your talisman periodically. They work like a battery and need to be charged and periodically drained.

4. Turn your talisman away from you when you are angry or sad so it doesn't absorb any negativity, but will, in a sense, carry your negativity away. Then refill it with your positive intention.

5. Consecration or sealing to one of the four elements: earth, air, fire, and water. Kind of like water is used with baptism, acting as an immediate water seal. Let your intuition guide you to your chosen element rather than a particular ritual. That way you have sealed your covenant between you and your talisman.

6. Recharge your talisman. Remember they are like your cell phone battery and need to be recharged. Use any of the previously mentioned methods, such as sage, candles, moonlight, etc. Take advantage of full moons, eclipses, rainwater, and herbs.

GROUNDING, CENTERING, & SHIELDING

If you are just starting out as a newbie witch, it is imperative that you learn these techniques before you start working magic.

Centering is the foundation of vibrational energy work, and therefore, of magic itself. Centering starts at the beginning of your magical work. If you have practiced meditation, this will be easier for you because it utilizes many of the same techniques.

- Find a comfortable place where you won't be disturbed. I have a small corner in my bedroom that I have made into a private little sanctuary for myself. It has a few candles, a big floor pillow, a small altar where I try to keep a few fresh cut flowers. Next, take several deep breaths, exhale slowly, and relax. Find a simple tone such as "Om" and chant for five minutes.
- Next, start to visualize energy by rubbing your hands together, warming them up. You will start to feel tingles in your hands. That is energy! You will soon be able to sense the energy you have created as if you are holding it in the palms of your hands, literally. I promise it works!
- With much practice you will learn how to shape and manipulate your ball of energy and create it whenever you need to feel centered.

Grounding is a method for getting rid of excess energy that may be stored up during your spell workings or rituals. There are times when anxiety kicks into high gear for all of us. Oddly, at times that anxiety produces a sense of heightened awareness, especially if you are centered first. It simply means that you have some excess energy you need to release.

- Use the same technique as you did for centering, but instead of drawing the energy inside of you, you want to push it out. Close your eyes and take your ball of energy and push it down into the ground, hence the term grounding. You can also push it into a tree or a bucket of water, or some other item that can absorb it. I take mine outside and throw it up in the air, sometimes. That way, I know I have gotten rid of it.

Shielding protects you from mental, magical, and psychic attacks. It's a strategy for creating an energy barrier around yourself that unwanted or unsavory people or spirits can't penetrate. You use your same ball of energy from the centering and grounding exercise, but when you are shielding, you are surrounding yourself by enveloping your entire body in it.

- Focus on your energy ball, and expand it outward, over your head, down to under your feet. In the same way you can cleanse yourself by burning a sage bundle, you're creating a protective shield. I have friends that are experts in reading auras, and they can tell when I have been shielding. "My, your aura is huge today," they say. Shielding comes in very handy if you know you are going to be in a group or with another person who drains you of your energy.

VISUALIZING

Developing your visualization skills allows you to create full images in your mind of people, places, events, and things. Picturing sounds, sights, tastes, and touch sensations in your mind manifests your intention through your senses. Picturing images in your mind's eye helps you to truly manifest your visions into a reality. For example, visualizing yourself getting hired for your dream job and that you've already received the job offer thrusts that power of positive thinking into a successful job interview.

Here are the steps for how to visualize:

1. Think about a time when you were content or happy.
2. Practice some deep breathing with your eyes closed.
3. Visualize yourself happy and safe. Remember the place, scene, smell, sounds, tastes, and feelings.
4. Perform visualization exercises before bedtime, during spiritual bathing, and just after you wake up. It will enhance your ability to connect to your unconsciousness.

MEDITATING

Meditation practices help to quiet the noisy chatter in your mind and access profound relaxation and spiritual connectedness. There are many benefits to meditation emotionally, physically, mentally, and spiritually. It reduces stress, relieves any aches and pains, and helps you gain access to your higher self and magical fortitude. Use mediation to guide your insight on how to communicate with the Universe, the Elements, nature, and your inner witch. Meditation is used in magical practice for spells, divination, and ritual.

Use the guided imagery tutorial I have provided or conduct a mantra meditation. Mantra meditation is deep breathing and humming. While humming, you become aligned with the cosmic energies that require a heightened state of awareness. With practice, you can train your brain to pick up on senses and perceptions not readily available during active consciousness. You can learn to flow in the direction of life without getting hung up on needless obstacles.

Most witches believe the harmony and vibrations of chanting certain syllables, such as "om" take you into a deeper meditative state. Diving deep into meditation helps to release any blocked or negative energy disrupting your well-being. You might choose a specific word or phrase that emphasizes your reasons for meditation, such as "peace" or "calm." I enjoy using words I like the sound of; for some reason, I chant "free and then dom." It just came out of me one time when I was a beginner witch and I still use it today. You can use it, too, or find a word that you can breathe out effortlessly and has meaning.

Some people like to use affirmation mantras, such as: "I have love for myself and others," or "I am at peace with the world," or "Each day is a new beginning."

Using affirmation mantras also enlightens you to your intentions. Don't get frustrated if you don't get immediate results. Just know that changes for the good are happening when you say kind words to yourself and ultimately will reflect your vision for your life and increase the chances of it becoming a reality.

Mantra meditation is also known as concentration mediation and here are the steps for you to practice:

1. Sit on a comfortable pillow (if you lay down you might fall asleep), wearing comfortable clothing, with your eyes closed.

2. Focus on your breathing. Notice the sensation of the air moving in and out, your chest rising and settling.

3. If you begin to feel distracted, calmly refocus your thoughts without feeling annoyed about getting distracted. Learning how to refocus will pay off big time in your spellcrafting.

   a. Note: You can also use words, prayers, sounds, or whispers repetitively.

RELAXING

The fact that stress and anxiety block the flow of positive energy and wreak havoc on our mental, physical, emotional, and spiritual health has been well established. They erode the quality of our lives. As a beginner witch, it is crucial for you to learn techniques for relaxation when preparing or spellwork or ritual. Relaxation methods such as deep breathing, guided imagery, and muscle relaxation will expose you to better focus and concentration on your abilities to manifest your intentions.

GUIDED IMAGERY

This is an example of how to learn to use guided imagery as a relaxation technique, trance technique, and meditative activity. I remember a time, some years ago, when there was a good deal of chaos happening all around me. I began having bouts of dysphoria and found focusing on my intuition difficult. However, I found a way to make life as beautiful as I imagined it could be.

BRIDGET'S BEACH GETAWAY: A GUIDED IMAGERY TUTORIAL

1. Find a comfortable place to sit or lie for thirty minutes undisturbed.
2. Take four deep breaths, in through your nose and out through your pursed lips.
3. Start at the top of your head (crown chakra) relaxing your eyebrows, then your nose and cheeks, next your tongue and lips. Continue by moving slowly down your neck, to your shoulders, and all the way to your tippy toes, concentrating on each group of muscles as you move down.

4. Feel the tension flowing out of your fingertips and the tips of your toes.

5. Enjoy the heaviness, feeling at ease, and being completely relaxed.

6. Let whatever you're sitting or lying on bear all of your weight, with no help from you.

7. Relax your mind, your chest, and each internal organ.

8. Now imagine yourself walking down the beach. The sound of the waves, the smell of the ocean air. Picture in your mind the salty breeze washing over you, as you continue to walk and enjoy each little critter, seagull, or starfish you see along the way.

9. Suddenly, you see in front of you, in the middle of the sand, an object. As you walk closer, you realize it is a raft.

10. As you walk up to the raft, you know that it is a magical raft.

11. With great peace and confidence, you slide your raft into the water and lay down on it. As you do this, the raft begins to slowly float and start moving across the water.

12. Everywhere you look is beautiful, smells beautiful, sounds beautiful, and feels beautiful.

13. You see the sunset, an infinite number of stars shine, the moon rising, all while you are floating relaxed.

14. Consider your life in a year from now, and how peaceful and relaxed you will be.

15. What does your life look like? Visualize an image of your life as pure happiness and positivity.
16. Visualize yourself in the places you love to be, such as in your garden, engaging with the Moon Goddess, watching your kids playing soccer. Whatever it is, it is wonderful.
17. Slowly, bring yourself back to the present.
18. Now you have a place to go whenever you feel tension.
19. For thirty minutes a day, take yourself back to your magic raft, and enjoy the ride.

SPIRITUAL BATHING

I like to take meditative showers with the intention of cleansing away any negative energy as the water pours over my body, down the drain any bad joujou flows. That is not the same as a spiritual bath. Spiritual bathing is a ritual that tends to your spiritual hygiene. They revitalize your energy centers or chakras, as well as refresh and rejuvenate you.

We all need to practice self-love. As a witchling, or new witch, start out by setting aside 30 minutes of uninterrupted peace. I can't reiterate enough that magic is all about setting your intention, and that includes spiritual bathing.

Here are the steps to guide you into the world of spiritual bathing techniques:

1. Clean the bathroom! Setting your space on

the sacred dial is important for all spell work, so clean the tub and counter tops, and make room for the items you want to surround yourself with for this ritual.

2. Make sure any items, such as crystals, herbs, oils, and candles are smudged or charged.

3. Choose a scent you want to be enveloped in during your bathing ritual. Make sure it is aligned with how you want to feel. For example, lavender brings peace, protection, better sleep, and happiness. Cinnamon and tea tree oil bring an energy boost.

4. Pick your candles, match the colors to your intention.

5. Sprinkle some pink Himalayan salt in the water, or float some rose petals. It's whatever makes you feel the way you want to feel.

6. Choose your sound. It can be your favorite music, or it could be calming meditation sounds. I recommend staying away from songs with lyrics, so you can focus on spiritual awareness.

7. Fill your tub with warm water deep enough to cover your shoulders.

Bath Ingredients

Salt: For clearing your energy, natural salt is the way to go. It has the power to release any type of negative debris mulling around your energy. I love natural sea salt, pink Himalayan salt, and Epsom salt, and they are all easy to come by. Never use table salt because it has been refined and many of the important minerals have been removed. Use about a handful of natural salt.

Baking Soda: Sodium ions mixed with bicarbonate dissolves in the bath water and has both spiritual and physical benefits. Use 1 cup.

Lavender: For some reason, in my opinion, lavender is the poster child for spiritual wellness. But whatever raises your spiritual awareness is the way to go. I like to boil the buds, if I have them; if not, I use my diffuser.

Carnations: To soothe a broken heart, boil some fresh red carnations, add some coconut milk, strain the fluid, and add it to your bath water.

Rose Water: For self-love. Float the petals on their own or boil them until there is no color left in the petals, then strain and add to your bath. The aroma of rose water makes you feel like you're giving yourself special attention.

Herbs: Herbs have so many benefits so choose which herbs suit your intention. Of course, you can't go wrong with basil or rosemary.

Once you have taken your ceremonial bathing ritual, you are ready for bedtime or for casting a circle and spellcrafting!

SLEEPING THE WITCHY WAY

A good night's sleep can never be underestimated, and that holds true for the vital role it plays within witchcraft! When the body and the mind are well rested, your energy levels improve, as do your intuitions and your abilities to receive dream messages. As your witchcraft matures, you will learn about sending your spirit on astral journeys while your physical body lies safely in your bed.

Not much is possible in witchcraft without proper rest. There are many methods for improving your sleeping habits, from getting a better quality of sleep or getting more of it. Witchy ways of sleeping are holistic by nature.

Here are a few helpful hints:

- No caffeinated beverages after 6 pm, for obvious reasons. Don't drink more than two cups of coffee per day, especially if you sweeten it, as your unstable blood sugars interfere with sleep. Overdoing it with caffeine doesn't allow you to stay attuned to your body or spirit as we don't know we're burnt out until it wears off.
- Don't eat your dinner too late. Eat your dinner at least four hours before sleep. Your body needs time and energy to digest your food; when you're full, it's busy digesting rather than helping you sleep. Falling asleep because you are so full is food sedation and not a natural form of sleep. But, having an apple with a spot of peanut butter as a bedtime snack can be comforting.
- Keep your bedroom on the cooler side, and dark, of course. If you are used to sleeping

with the light on, try to get unused to it. Light stimulates your nervous systems, so even when your eyes are shut, a light source can interrupt your sleep. It is harder to cool your body down than to warm it up, but keep the room temperature that is comfortable for you.

- Only use your bed for the 2 S's: sleeping and sex. No video games, TV, or study time. That way, your brain will only associate your bed with sleeping. Sleeping routines set the quality of your sleep. I've been there with, "Just one more game, and then I'll go to sleep...well, maybe one more..."

- Prepare your bedroom. Make it as clutter-free as possible, with as few electronics as possible, and as clean as possible.

- Crystals provide soothing energies to help you sleep. Selenite cleanses the room, and an amethyst under your pillow will offer peaceful slumber. If you have nightmares or night terrors, keep a rose quartz close by.

- An hour or so before bedtime, light a salt lamp. They purify the air and lower the energy levels in the room. Sometimes too much energy in a room keeps us awake.

- Start relaxing an hour before bedtime. That means no screens, exercise, or bright lights.

- This routine is referred to as proper sleep hygiene, and takes about a month for your brain to code it as such. Habits can take a while to form, but good ones bring long-term benefits. Practice good sleep hygiene until it is ingrained in your brain.

- Note: Some mediations are stimulating so choose wisely. Meditation sounds will teach you how to relax and with time you will be able to cue your body to relax without the sound.
- Journaling can be a yay or a nay. If you tend to ruminate or you have something troubling on your mind, write it out, and get it out of your system so you can sleep. It is nay, if you like to write stories where your imagination takes off and keeps you awake.

CASTING A CIRCLE

Casting or opening and closing a circle is a ritual for thanking and showing respect to the Elements for helping you to draw in their energy and release it.

Step-by-Step Instructions on How to Cast a Circle

1. Sweep your sacred space with your besom or broom, making sure it is thoroughly cleansed, and then smudge the entire area with sage.
2. Place a candle or a crystal (already charged) in each of the four cardinal directions. If you are calling on the fifth element Spirit, draw a pentacle either with chalk or salt and place

your candles or crystals on each of the five points.

3. Once you draw your circle to the size you want it and step inside, do not step out until the ritual is complete.

4. Step inside of your circle and face the East and call upon the Element Water.

5. Continue to move clockwise (deosil or sunward) and call upon each element. "I call upon you, Earth, etc.)

6. Enter a trance or meditative state until you are centered and grounded.

7. Visualize a connection with each of the four or five elements, imagining how they feel around you and on your body: water swishing, the breeze of the wind, the warmth of the sun's fire, and the cool earth under your feet. (I love to be barefoot.)

8. Complete your circle facing north.

9. You are now ready for ritual or spell casting.

10. Close the circle when you're finished by paying respect and expressing your gratitude to the Elements and whatever deities you invited.

11. One by one, pick up each representative candle, crystal, etc. and finally undo the circle bidding farewell to each of the elements out loud and with great sincerity moving in a counterclockwise movement. That is casting in reverse and closing your circle.

A frequently asked question that comes up in my group sessions with new witches is how to dispose of ritual items or offerings made during the ceremony once the ritual has concluded. It is a very good question. There are various methods for disposing of ritual items after a spell, but there are a few things to consider. Some traditions have requirements for the disposal of ritual times. Also, consider what the item is made of. Is it organic? Is it the disposal part of the spell?

Let's discuss some of the ways you can dispose of your ritual items and get you one step closer to becoming a magical practitioner.

1. Burning uses the power of fire. Almost every ritual item can be disposed of by using the power of fire and is often considered part of the spell or ritual itself. It is the best way to destroy the object's influence and can be burned as part of the ceremony. You can burn offerings such as meat and bread or anything you want to be rid of permanently. It is a good way to make sure it will never return.

2. Water and Earth: If your ritual offering is organic, such as vegetables, tobacco, fruits, blood, or plant materials, you can bury it in the earth. You can even bury it in your garden. As the organic material decomposes, it fertilizes the land. It is a great way to give

back and continue the cycle of life. If you are buying incense ashes or candle stubs, only do it in your own yard. You can also throw organic materials into a moving body of water, but it has to be organic!

3. Sharing with the animals: Let's say you used nuts and seeds in your spell or ritual. As long as they have not been chemically treated in any way, scatter them for the squirrels, birds, and any local critters hanging around. I know a few green witches that make offerings to grain gods, so they are always feeding the ducks, squirrels, birds, and other feathery friends who eat it, and the cycle of life of the grain goes on. If you have to dispose of water, flowers, or herbs, you can leave them there, they will blow away and find a new home.

V

SPELLS FOR BEGINNERS

I wanted to include some simple spells to get you started. A warning to not expect dramatic results the first few times you cast a spell. Your results will improve with time and practice. Now that you know the basics for becoming a newbie witch, you certainly have much to consider. It's time to tap into your life and tap into your supernatural self and start working magic. The manifestations of your magical workings will improve your psychic abilities and solve many difficult situations in your life. With these easy-to-learn spells and the best and most powerful witchcraft rituals, you will be able to make the right decision and transform your life and the lives of your loved ones to a happier and healthier quality of life.

HONEY AND HERB SPELL FOR DRAWING LOVE

This spell can be about someone you want to draw into your life but haven't had the courage to do anything about it or it could be someone from your past that you are longing to reconnect with. Maybe you're lonely and can't stand the thought of lying in bed at night alone and simply want some human warmth. Love spells like this one are usually about romantic love, but they can also help to sweeten your relationships with friends, family, co-workers, or to improve your overall experiences with others.

This is one of the first spells I created some time ago, and it has really stood the test of time. Honey has been used for centuries because of its sweetness. I love it because honey is the one organic item that can never spoil or go bad. The characteristic of sweetness is a powerful ingredient for conflict resolution, a sense of bonding, and its generation of affection.

WHEN TO PERFORM THE SPELL:

Anytime or New Moon

HOW LONG IT TAKES:

20-30 minutes

WHAT YOU'LL NEED:

A pen and paper
Jar of honey (Orange Blossom or Clover)
Red Candle
1 Basil leaf

STEPS

1. Write the person's name you want to attract three times on the paper in succession.
2. Next, turn the paper sideways and write your own three times in succession, crossing over the letters of the other person's name.
3. Write down in cursive your intention exactly the way you want it to be manifested without lifting your pen in a circle around both names. Don't even stop to dot your i's and cross your t's. Do that after you complete the circle.
4. Put the basil leaf on top of the circle.

5. Fold the paper in half and then in half again with the basil leaf tucked inside.

6. Push the paper down into the honey, making sure to coat your fingers. Leave the paper in the honey.

7. While your fingers are still in the honey chant: *Honey Bee, You and Me, Take my Hand, Our Love to Be. No Longer Far, I've raised the Bar, and Sealed it in this Honey Jar.*

8. Remove your fingers and glide your tongue across your sticky fingers, while picturing the lips of the one you desire.

9. Seal the jar.

10. Place your red candle on the top of the lid and let it melt, spilling down the sides of the jar.

11. Repeat step 10 once a week until you have drawn your love interest to you. It should only take a couple of weeks, and that's if you haven't met the person yet.

BUILD A BOWL PROSPERITY SPELL

Building a prosperity bowl was one of the first spells I learned. It is a great newbie witch's spell if, like most of us, you wouldn't mind some extra cash in your pocket. It also leaves you with something to admire and remind you of your intention set for the spell. The great news is that the spell works fantastically, as long as you understand that for the spell to work, so do you. Stay keen on opportunities that come your way after casting the spell. Trusting always that your spell is working, follow its guidance toward the goals that will surely be laid out in front of you.

WHEN TO PERFORM THE SPELL:

Any time during a waxing moon

HOW LONG IT TAKES:

As long as it takes the candle to burn down

CHANT:

Prosperity grows as money flows,
My bank account is starting to glow,
For in this bowl abundance shows
Crystals and coins and it grows
As it is and should be.

WHAT YOU'LL NEED:

A bowl
Pink Himalayan salt and water
Crystals: Green Aventurine, Citrine, Jade
Add any other green colored crystals
Silver colored coins and any loose change
Cinnamon, basil, dried orange peel
Bay leaf and a Pen
Green Candle
Abalone Shell

STEPS

1. Cleanse your bowl with pink Himalayan salt water.
2. Pick up each item and charge them with your intentions by holding or rolling them around in your hands.
3. Carefully place your candle in the middle of the bowl.
4. Add your chosen items to the bowl one at a

time, holding them between your hands and charging them with your intentions.

5. Light your candle.
6. Write your intention on your bay leaf and light it on fire, and place it lit in your abalone shell, sending your intention up into the Universe in a string of smoke.
7. Let the candle burn all the way down.
8. Place the bowl in the prosperity corner of your home, the back left-hand corner.
9. Each day reflect on your intention while feeding it coins for a regular spell boosting energy.
10. You can keep it going as long as you want and watch your bank account grow. It is also a great piggy bank.

SEE YA SPELL FOR BANISHING SOMEONE

I f you have frenemies, mean gossipers, or even enemies in your life, it's time to take back your emotions, reputation, and all of that wasted energy. This a spell not only banishes but protects by using mirrors, sympathetic magic, and black salt to reflect the negativity as it's happening and to block it from causing you any more harm.

Sympathetic magic uses connections and corre-spondences between your intention and non-magical objects, such as poppets. Sympathetic magic can be learned even as a beginner. With practice, you will learn how to manifest the ability to psychically enter into another person's or creature's state of mind.

WHEN TO PERFORM THE SPELL:

Saturday, full or waxing moon

HOW LONG IT TAKES:

As long as it takes the candle to burn down

CHANT:

I banish you by the powers of the Universe
My soul and your soul to never traverse
I banish you by the powers of the stars
Your path and my path will be afar
As it is and should be

WHAT YOU'LL NEED:

1 piece Parchment Paper
Black Ink
Black Salt (mix sage burnings with salt)
Mirror
Bowl
Sage

STEPS

1. Smudge your sacred space with sage.
2. Cast a sacred circle.
3. Chant the above mantra charging your intention while writing down the full name of the person.
4. Put their name in the bowl and cover it with black salt.

5. Put a mirror on top of the paper and visualize all of their negativity reflecting back onto them.
6. Close the Circle.
7. Finish the spell by burying all of the contents far from your home.
8. Make sure to cleanse the mirror thoroughly and store it for another spell.

LUCKY ME SPELL

Wind chimes, candles, pendants, four-leaf clovers, crystals, herbs, acorns, elephants with their trunks turned up, and essential oils have been used throughout history as good luck charms.

Essential Oils for good luck:

1. Healthy: Grapefruit oil attracts uplifting and healthy vibes.
2. Travel: Orange oil carries with it the luck of St. Christopher and St. Patrick, as well as energizing your day.
3. Romance: Ylang Ylang will put you and your partner in the mood.
4. Money: Lemongrass essential oil.
5. Career: Tea Tree and Rosemary essential oils stimulate concentration and memory.
6. Reputation: Peppermint is mentally

stimulating and gives you confidence for when you are counting on having a good reputation to carry you through.

7. Romance and Family: Lavender is calming.

Good luck spells with candle burning rituals have historically been used as powerful white magic rituals. White magic only uses positive energies that cannot cause any harm to others. If you're feeling down on your luck and need that quick boost, casting candle spells is sure to get you back on the road to good fortune.

Good luck spellcasting with candle magic is perfect for the beginner witch. As with all spells you should cast a good luck spell as if it has already manifested. It is imperative that you have an optimistic attitude down into the very depths of your soul, so mediating for a good fifteen minutes about your intention prior to casting the spell is the best idea.

I offer this spell to anyone who wants good luck in love, money, and employment. If you are looking for good luck in money or prosperity, use a green candle. Choose a candle size that accounts for the time it takes to burn all the way down. For romance and love luck use a pink candle, and for loyalty in your relationship use a white and a pink candle.

WHEN TO PERFORM THE SPELL:

Saturday, full or waxing moon

HOW LONG IT TAKES:

As long as it takes the candle to burn down

CHANT:

*Money, money, money come to me. It is
my will. As it is and should be.*

or
*Luck in love, come to me. It is
my will. As it is and should be.*

or
*Wonderful job, come to me. It is
my will. As it is and should be.*

WHAT YOU'LL NEED:

Votive Candle and holder
Lighter or matches
Virgin olive oil to dress candle
Athame or knife

STEPS

1. Light the candle corresponding with your
   intention while chanting the mantra that is
   associated with the luck you desire.

2. Visualize the good luck you will have from this day forward.
3. Let the candle(s) burn all the way down.

HEALTH AND HEALING SPELL JAR

Spell jars and spell bottles have been a magical practice fixture since ancient times. These are great spells because you can accomplish their magic as a beginner, they are personal, and they're self-contained. As you now know, there are many ways to practice your craft, and the same goes for crafting a spell jar or spell bottle.

When I make spell bottles, I like to use corked tops, but any lid will do. While choosing your vessel, think about your materials, where your jar or bottle is going to either be displayed or not on display, and your assembling preference. If you are going to be using fluids or liquids, you may want to use a jar or a larger mouthed bottle. If you plan on disposing your materials after your spell is complete, you'll want to use a biodegradable container. Whichever vessel you do choose, it has to be thoroughly cleansed before you start to add anything into it. You can smudge it, cleanse it with sunlight, wash it out with a nice lavender soap, and make a ritual out of the cleansing process, too.

If your spell has a target outcome, begin with a taglock or token, such as photos, a lock of hair, a piece of fabric, or even their name written down on a bay leaf or a piece of paper. Then choose your dry ingredients, items, or materials. Always lean on your intuition. You may have very personal relationships with certain herbs, crystals, colors, coins, and other materials you want for your bottle or jar.

Choose objects you want to represent your spell's intention and how to symbolize it. If it is a protection spell jar, for instance, you might include pieces of a snail's shell, turtle's shell, or seashell. A spell for transformation could use snakeskin or butterfly wings.

For the fluids or liquids, use vinegar, olive oil, honey, or moon blessed water. I have a spell bottle with moon blessed water and my favorite healing gems. I have it out on display because it came out so beautiful. Of course, some of us throw a shot of tequila in there, too! Just make sure the lip or cork is on tight.

Always speak incantations of your intention over and into your bottle and jar. You can then seal it by dripping and overlapping generous layers of wax over the lid. That can be a ritual within itself, too, and adds power to your jar or bottle spells. It also seals in your spell. Next, activate your spell with either your incantations or some spells call for shaking. Some of my witchy friends believe that the ritual of sealing with candle wax also activates the spell.

WHEN TO PERFORM THE SPELL:

The waning moon, if you can wait.

HOW LONG IT TAKES:

As long as it takes the candle to burn down

CHANT:

With the love in my soul
Good health and a healing goal;
Water, Fire, Earth, and Air,
Help him/her have no pain to bear
Make (name) as healthy as can be
This is my will, as it is and should be

WHAT YOU'LL NEED:

Small square of white cloth
Bay leaves (for strength)
Carnation petals
Mint (for vitality)
Sea salt (for cleansing)
Tiger's Eye stone (for protection)
Blessed or moon-charged water
Sage
One white candle
Soil

STEPS

1. Center and ground yourself.
2. On the piece of cloth, write the full name of the person you or yours.
3. On your altar, place your spell jar in the center, and the blessed water, soil, sage, and one white candle to represent the elements around it.
4. While you are chanting the above mantra, slowly start placing each ingredient into your jar.
5. Seal your jar.
6. Leave it out under the waning moonlight and after for seven days.
7. Each night conduct your incantation over your jar.
8. Once the person is healed, bury the jar, and thank the deities and Elements for their help.

BRIDGET'S INTUITION BOOSTING SPELL

WHEN TO PERFORM THE SPELL:

The waning moon

HOW LONG IT TAKES:

As long as it takes the candle to burn down

CHANT:

My intuition is the key
to provide the clarity that I need
Crystals vibrate in my hands
They me wisdom from the land
Confusion in my mind be gone
From this silver knowledge dawns
Make my aurora a happy glow
From within I will know
As it is and should be

WHAT YOU'LL NEED:

Moonstone crystal
One quarter
One Indigo candle
Rose quartz crystal
Rosemary

STEPS:

1. Smudge the area and sit in a comfortable position.
2. Anoint your indigo candle with rosemary oil.
3. Light the candle.
4. Place the moonstone crystal in one hand and the rose quartz in the other hand and place your hands in your lap.
5. Place the quarter on your altar between you and the candle, representing a symbolic connection of the elements from the flame to your body.
6. Close your eyes, center yourself, and repeat the chant three times.
7. Spend five minutes in total stillness listening to your intuition.
8. Let the candle burn all the way down or snuff it out if you want to repeat the spell.

CONDUCTING A NATURE RITUAL

1. Find a natural setting away from all humans where you can relax. The forest, beach, mountains, caves, or in a meadow, anywhere you can connect with the Elements.
2. While relaxing, take in your environment and start shifting your focus from human centeredness to Nature centeredness.
3. Create a dialog with yourself, reminding you that you are part of the circle of life, part of this natural setting, part of nature, and that your reason for your visit is to become one with nature and to nourish your spirit.
4. Picture in your mind Mother Nature's arms wrapped around you like an ancient tree, as you notice the Earth, the air, and the sky providing you with spiritual energy.
5. Express your gratitude to the planet, the celestial realm, and the Elements for their care to all forms of life.
6. Look around at each plant and pick one to focus on. Touch it. Smell it. Taste its essence and enter a trance of being one with that particular plant.
7. Slowly bring yourself out of the trance and back into human form.
8. Thank the plant out loud for being your friend, your teacher, your family.
9. Meditate on your spiritual time as a plant.
10. Next, move your thoughts to the life

surrounding your plant, and visualize yourself every bit as much a part of nature as the plant.

11. Realize you are related to the birds, the wind, the water, and the animals.

12. Focus on the patterns, the four cardinal directions, the wind's rhythms, and the colors.

13. Take a snapshot of your new spiritual sanctuary so you can return anytime you wish while meditating.

REVERSE A CURSE BELL SPELL

Bells are often overlooked as powerful magical instruments. Its main purpose in magic is for breaking curses, ridding a space of negative energy, removing a spell, and for protection spells. This is how bells became traditional for weddings, because they drive away unwanted energies.

WHEN TO PERFORM THE SPELL:

When needed

HOW LONG IT TAKES:

A few minutes

WHAT YOU'LL NEED:

2 Bells (Any bell with a clapper)
2 Hands

STEPS

1. Cross your hands at the wrist in front of you at the waist holding your bells.
2. Raise your hands over your head and slip them apart as you bring them around to your sides making the bells ring.

NEW JOB SPELL

New job searches can be frustrating and leave you feeling defeated. As always, a bit of magic infused with your intent to be newly employed is yours for the asking. This is a wonderful spell that will help you achieve your goal of finding that dream job, efficiently and quickly. Here's a spell with a money oil recipe bonus. Why buy money oil from a mystic when you can easily make your own? Before casting this New Job Spell, visualize what your job will be, so the magical energy knows where to go to sweeten your life and attract success.

WHEN TO PERFORM THE SPELL:

When applying for a new job

HOW LONG IT TAKES:

15 Minutes

WHAT YOU'LL NEED:

White Candle
Candle holder
Athame
Job application

Money Oil Recipe:

Grapeseed oil base
Add: cinnamon, mint
basil, nutmeg, and bay leaf

STEPS:

1. Carve the name of the company in the candle.
2. Dress the candle wiping money oil toward you.
3. Place a copy of your job application under your candle holder.
4. Light the candle while picturing your congratulations letter welcoming you to your first day at work.

CONCLUSION

There are so many reasons why people are drawn to the art of nature-centered magical practice and even more reasons why they choose to change their lifestyle to take the journey of the witch. The information you have read here gives you an advantageous starting point and an informed, positive direction to go from here.

While this short book is only a taste of what a life of magic can do for you, I hope it encourages you to seek out more knowledge about witchcraft, expand your psychic abilities, broaden your horizons, and learn what it means to live the life of a witch. With magic, the possibilities are endless, and developing an intimate relationship with your materials, the elements, and your higher-self is a complex work of art that includes casting your first spells, learning to center and ground yourself, cleansing and charging your sacred space, developing what you want your altars to represent, casting a circle, and so much more.

We learn very early in life that failure is how we learn. If I tried to count the number of spells that didn't seem to work for me when I first started out, the list would be a long one. In the beginning, my spell work was great, but my execution didn't quite account for the loopholes. Not focusing on the importance of being centered and grounded, forgetting to smudge or cleanse a sacred space are some biggies to account for. It's easy to get caught up in the ceremonial aspects of witchcraft rather than focusing on the magic. It is and should be a most enjoyable process, but if you find yourself trying to graduate to the next level, you are missing the best part of the journey: Finding out who *you* are.

Cultivating your relationship with the Universe doesn't happen overnight. Stay your course and enjoy the learning part more than the end result and you will find a line of open communication with everything cosmic and celestial. Don't be surprised to find out that the universe responds to exactly what you tell it, so what you don't say matters just as much. After all of these years of loving my craft, I rarely fail in spell work. The reason is that I learned from those failures I had as a newbie, and then integrated my new knowledge into the next step toward my journey to have more effective outcomes.

Life these days is a digital and fast-paced existence which if we're not careful can disconnect us from the spiritual realm and the natural order of things. I hope this book nourished your body, mind, and spirit, in a way that welcomes you to the wonderful world of witchcraft. Witches don't have a color, shape, race, or specific religion. We come from all walks of life. For me, it is a lifestyle of peace and harmony with all things natural.

By reading this book you have been introduced to the practical applications of ancient philosophies and given the tools you need to harness your inner-witch and improve your happiness, confidence, and wellbeing. I wanted to share my in-depth education and understanding of the magical culture of witchcraft so you, too, can know how to transform your life through spiritual connectedness and enlightenment.

Ultimately, I hope that what you do with this book is create your own magical style, using these spells and explanations as templates to cultivate your own particular talents: there is nothing more powerful than exploring your own particular abilities and personal correspondences to discover just how potent your own brand of magic can be. As a beginner, starting to trust your own intuitions will help you to identify what magical tools work best for you. As long as you practice your magic with clear intentions and positive motives, your spells will become more potent, and your results more assured. Conjure up some self-love, good luck, and purpose today!

Made in United States
Troutdale, OR
09/09/2023

12747264R00066